Growing Out Of It

A self-portrait by
Oliver Megan Jean Roweth,
ages 12-18

First edition, published in Australia in 2026 by
Oliver Roweth, oliverroweth.com

ISBN: 978-0-646-73547-4

For cataloguing: Library and educational institutions
should consult standard cataloguing services for
subject headings and classification.

10 9 8 7 6 5 4 3 2 1
First printing: March 2026

Cover art by Oliver Roweth

Author's note

The writing of *Growing Out Of It* has taken almost six years, and most of it was done before I really knew what it was going to become. I only realised in 2025 that what I had, scattered between various files, notes, and setlists, was approaching a collection. All that was left by then was to order that poetry into a story, fill in the gaps, and work out how to publish a book.

Throughout that process, and long before it began, I have been lucky to be supported and inspired by a variety of wonderful people. The bush poetry community has been there for me since I was perching on plastic chairs to reach the mic, and I never would have made it even that far without my amazing family. I want to give special thanks to Kim Kelly for her incredibly generous help with publishing this book – it would have been stapled cardboard and paper without her.

Before you read on, please note that this collection includes discussion of death, suicidal ideation, queerphobia, and ableism, as well as graphic depictions of gender dysphoria, periods and the generally traumatising experience of being young and marginalised. Spoiler alert: I make it through. I'm here publishing this, after all.

*This is for my family, who taught me how to live,
and for my partners and friends, who reminded me I wanted to,
but mostly, it's for you.*

Good luck out there.

Act I

Act II

Act III

Act IV

Act I

contains suicidal ideation, ableism,
and gender dysphoria

Passive Suicidal Ideation

to be or not to be –
that *is* the question
how comforting to know
that years and years before
a little girl sat on the edge of a sandpit
genuinely considering every alternative
to another cross-country race
someone else was wondering the same

she hasn't stopped wondering
even fifteen seems so far away
and tomorrow will bring
well
more of this, probably
more inexplicable wrongness
more hours on the shower floor
more hiding her chest in the change rooms

she's cutting up the onions for dinner
they're stinging her eyes
and the knife is very sharp, very there
just there
and she doesn't know yet
that there's a future worth waiting for
but she wouldn't want her sister to find her

for now, that'll have to be enough

Introductions

what does it feel like?
it's everybody's favourite question
and they'll ask it like it's smalltalk
how does it feel, when your brain works like that?

and I say, it feels fast, feels cluttered, feels colourful
feels like a thousand things at once
feels like air tastes, too everpresent to note-
what does *your* brain 'feel like'? could you tell me?

it's less about how your brain feels
and more about how living does
more about the way the world responds to you
brain-in-a-meatsuit that you are

about a teacher asking
how much time you waste a day
and you sitting there with your hour of 'shower collateral'
wondering who she thinks she's talking to

about the way people tell you how nice it is
to see you with your headphones off
finally spending some time with us
while you barely register a word through the emptiness

about the girl, two years younger than you,
who you ask to move so you can plug your laptop in
softly asking if that helped, if you're okay
seeing some five-year-old in your shoes

I mean, I'm the one with the empathy problems
how do you think it feels?
why don't you just ask me my favourite colour
and we'll see how it goes from there?

Apologies

sometimes I wish I could speak
in words that actually explain
strip everything else away
and the words themselves wouldn't be so complicated:

I feel bad all the time but I don't cry very often, and
I yelled at you because I couldn't work out
how else to make you go away, and
I didn't mean to make us late,
I just couldn't get out of bed
until the number on the clock was right

except somewhere between my mouth and your ears
it goes wrong
and suddenly I'm just saying
I don't care

so
I'm sorry I didn't cry
when your dog died
but I stayed up late after you left
even though I never found a way to tell you

if a tree falls in the forest and it doesn't make a sound
does it matter that there's nobody around to hear?

Gender in the key of Autism

when I was six,
I knew I was a girl
the way I knew I was meant to sit crosslegged –
because they split the class down the middle
and I went on the left

when I was twelve,
I knew I was a girl
the way I knew it was weird that all my friends weren't –
because I spent so much time dodging probing questions
and defending a hatred of pink

I was fourteen before I realised
I only thought I was a girl
the way I'd thought I was straight –
sure, people kept telling me what a lovely young woman I was
but I've never been that good at picking up on social cues

still not straight, though
sorry about that
sorry about the new pronouns,
and the name change,
and the flannel shirt I stole from you, dad,
however well it suits me

I was also fourteen before I realised
most girls don't struggle to stand in a crowded corridor
it's not just that I suck at coping
most girls don't even want to be boys, let alone cats
or at least still allowed to run around shirtless

so when I tell you to just call me *he*
or maybe *it*
or *they*, if those are too hard
it means
  sometimes I feel like a little more or less than a person
it means
  certainly I feel far less like a girl than a human being
it means
  god, please stop noticing how all my carefully scripted greetings
                                        take the shape of a curtsy
habits this old are hard to break

but I learned to be a girl the way I learned to be human –
imperfectly
frantically
learning my lines onstage
still shoving myself into a costume
a pair of shoes that chafed my heels
and a blonde wig

so,
sorry for the trouble,
sorry I'm late to it,
sorry I didn't like the pink wrapping paper
or the barbies your parents bought for my sixth birthday
because all they knew about me
was the *miss megan roweth* on the invite,
and sorry I couldn't tell you why

but hey, I'll take the nail polish
if you're still offering?

A poem about redecorating my bedroom (and nothing else)

redecorating is really fun, actually
once you get past the nervousness

y'know, the
   what if I mess it up?
   what if I pick the wrong colours? toss the wrong furniture?
   what if it turns out awful and then I have to live here?

but you're living here anyway
and right now you hate the wallpaper
you've outgrown the bed sheets
nothing is where you expect it to be
and you're already stuck with it

so why not?

I started temporary
cautious
a few posters
paintings and sketches
things I could take down
if I didn't really like them

but I *really* liked them
found myself pausing, smiling
just staring at my walls
instead of burying my head in books
trying not to notice them pressing in

I accelerated quickly
repainting the door
reorganising the bookshelves
making room on the desk for picture frames
and painting bold swirls of colour over the ceiling

and suddenly I could *breathe*
I could fill my lungs up
and open my eyes
and exist
in my own space
for the first time

I don't think I could survive going back
I'm making plans to paint my whole wall
moving the bed away
picking my colours
calling in consultants

and they always ask,
  aren't you nervous?
  are you sure?
  aren't you a little young
  to be changing things you'll be stuck with forever?

but that wallpaper is driving me crazy
and hey
aren't I stuck with it already?

Work In Progress

there's an art to self-creation
you start at imitation
a reflex, a tapped-knee spasm –
I want to be like that

but a boy is something you weren't
and a girl is something you aren't
and you're not sure where that leaves you,
untitled sculpture of meat and bone

meat and bone is not enough
steal language in fragments
build something out of it
not a self, not yet

just a vision board of splinters
disjointed, cobbled together
none of it quite *fits*
but you might learn to like the contrast

it's time to grow up
your body won't do it for you
good luck

Act II

Statistical Analysis

in highschool, I started to work myself out
the way teenagers tend to
I bought pins, changed my labels
and tried not to think about statistics

I am trying to write this into a poem
to make it feel profound, or justify the ink it's wasting
to explain it in a way that feels more like reality
than some strange dystopian fiction

but in highschool, I worked out my style
I had a first crush, a first kiss
I told my parents about the life I wanted to live
and I watched my life expectancy drop

On conscription

I wish sometimes
that I could have opted in

I would have
I swear I would
I *hope* I would

but I fall in love
like any fool might
and this is a statement

I want to get married one day
to the people I love
and this is a political aspiration

I live in my body
because there is nowhere else to go
and this is an ideology
or a movement
or a trend

we go home after the protest
we live through our next days
I go home
I keep living
this is a rebellion

History

they can never capture the paranoia
it's always the part they don't quite get
in the stories, the poetry
the trying-too-hard TV shows

because you just can't tell
who's gonna start looking at you
like you've *confessed* to something
and it's a lot worse than a boyfriend, or a chest binder

you never know
who you need to tiptoe around with half-truths
'my partner and my best friend' –
in the historical sense, I mean

historical- history, because it's over
forgotten about, wiped out
left to fiction
set back when those things really happened

my people are mentioned exactly twice
in my history textbook
both times, we are 'homosexuals'
in a bracketed list of the massacred

but hey, at least now we can get legally married
and then never tell a soul
unless we know which newspapers they read
and we're *sure*

lucky us, good thing it's over
those damn barbarians in the olden days
who'd kill a man for existing
are, of course, all dead and gone

and I'm sure, if I checked
my life expectancy would be just the same as yours
and if I wanted to plan a holiday
I could go anywhere I liked

and if I walked into a servo at 10pm
wearing clothes that fit me right
and used my own damn name to order a coffee-
I'd be perfectly safe

I'd be safe, the way everybody is so ready to promise
right up until I exist in front of them
and they realise
I do seem a little weird, after all

see, those inalienable rights we're all supposed to have
just go flying out the window
when you break the contract
and stop counting as human

but hey, if I make it through the years-long waiting list
for the changes I want *and* the ones I don't
I can change my legal gender to something else I'm not
and throw a fucking party

Shark Week

once a month
I wake up to bloody thighs
ruined sheets
a crime scene in my bedroom
so I get up, go to school, and pretend
I'm not being stabbed in the gut all day

stay calm, smile awkwardly,
and walk into the girls' bathrooms
for the first time in a month

I feel myself bleeding out
my body demanding of me motherhood
conscripting me to service
as I change my pads and fix my sheets and tell myself
three more years
while my insides peel off and drip out of me

my body is betraying me
I am far too late to stop it
and I cannot yet consent to assistance

I strip my shirt off
don't look in the mirror, don't look down
step out of the shower, wrap a towel around my waist-
and then remember
three more years
and hide from myself in the biggest hoodie I own

I buy my shirts three sizes up
I crush my chest until my ribs ache
and I wait

Testimony

once upon a time,
we tried to measure the weight of a soul
by weighing a living man
and waiting
and weighing his corpse to find the difference

21 grams seems a little light to me

my soul doesn't have a gender
my soul was not created to fit a closed system
my soul sits in my chest
immeasurable and unlabelled
but *this question may not be left blank*
and my best option is to get in first

to be clear
I am not allowed to get in first
my answers must line up with databases
filled out before my eyes could open
helpfully stripping me bare
mapping the topography of my body
for every boss, every teacher,
every cop who sees my paperwork

it is, of course, vital information
I cannot be allowed to enter a bathroom
until I clarify the dimensions of my chest
or at least what I intend to make them
or at least the gender of my soul

maybe my soul *is* a boy
I can't prove it isn't
maybe my soul is a girl
but it wants you to call it something else

maybe my soul is a poet
maybe my soul is a thunderstorm
maybe my soul is slowly cracking open
leaking blood and hope and love onto the pavement
as the world keeps demanding answers it can't give
and I can't make it stop-

and maybe I just think 'boyfriend' sounds cuter
would that make mine a liar, when he calls me his?
would that give you the right
to snatch the word back out my mouth
like something stolen?
will you bring the jury in
and call my soul to testify?

once upon a time,
we tried to measure the weight of a soul
here is how we cross-examine one:
on a scale of one to ten,
how much does it hurt
when I do *this*?

if you have above a seven,
you're allowed to fix yourself

I do not want to fix myself
I want to fix the world
I want a generation
who choose their language
and shape their bodies
by what they *want*
instead of what they can prove is agony
by measuring the immeasurable

but that's too hard to imagine
isn't it?

far easier:
a mismatch between soul and body
a flaw in my construction
irrespective of context
with no further implications

then it's a problem with a solution
or a tragic fatal flaw
or a bug in a functional system

then it simply requires medical intervention
before the movie can end
with my soul in line with my sex
and your dissonance corrected
and my clothes tight in the right places
and an M on the paperwork

it is impossible to quantify the nature of a soul
it is possible to define a social construct
it is possible to change one

still
if the burden of proof is on me
I have plenty of agony to demonstrate

does it come from the gender of my soul?

sure

whatever you need me to say

Women and Non-Men

there is a room
and you are outside it
you are hovering in the doorway

the girl on stage is talking
about seasons taking root under skin
and you think you can feel them there
twisting between your veins
choking them out until your fingertips turn black

she's talking about the cycles of the moon
the divine feminine
in tune with nature and connected to the earth

right now it mostly just seems like blood
blood on your legs
on your hands
on the tiles in the shower
hastily scrubbed off the sink
human tissue peeling off your insides
sticking to hair you refuse to shave
in rebellion and desperate conformity
staining you red

you do not want to be a goddess
but if this is not poetry
it cannot be anything but blood

there is a room
and you are outside it

there is a room with a locked door
and a room down the hall
with another locked door

there are rooms
and share-houses
and meeting halls
and not a single one will admit you have nowhere else to go

they have reason to be cautious
you know
of course you do
you're a boy when you can sell it
but you don't walk alone after dark

there's a kind of solidarity in that
the shared unsafety of a herd of deer
poised to bolt

men are a common enemy
and you are a wolf in deer's clothing

you are living inside a girl you have killed
a girl you are trying to kill
your relatives remember her fondly
as her death throes stain your thighs red
and you twist in her corpse like a chrysalis

there is a room
and you are outside it

even from here you swear they can smell the blood on your hands

27

Echolocation

I am thinking about echolocation

I am thinking about making noise in a dark room
trying to find the shapes in it
hoping to hear something back

I am thinking about poetry

I am thinking about attempts made to measure souls
to catalogue what cannot be catalogued
to set it all down on paper

I am thinking about getting frustrated in class
when I was old enough to know the answer
but not to spell the words

I am thinking about high school projects
butchered mannequins
slashed-out girlhood
collages of diagnostic paperwork
and the grades I got for them

I am thinking about dissection

I am thinking about how to lay out all the mess inside me
so somebody else can understand
so somebody else can be understood

I am thinking about art

I am thinking about sympathy
and how we talk about winning it
and how hard it is to sound innocent
even when you are

I am thinking about thinking about killing myself
and how often I said it out loud

I am thinking about statistics

I am wondering if every poem I have ever written
has been a puppy-eyed plea
a helpless raising of empty hands

I am wondering if all I'm ever saying
is *please don't shoot*

Act III

Temple

my body is a temple
I have been told this
for centuries we have insisted
these are holy things

these ribs, the rafters
this flesh, the sturdy walls
these sharp teeth, these soft fingertips,
place and method of worship

my body is not a site of silent sacrifice
not a place for confession,
repentance, and forgiveness
it is my home

I eat, I sleep, I laugh
I breathe in and out and in
I keep myself well
my halls alight with love and laughter

this is my hearthside
my canvas
my sanctuary
this is my resting place

my body is a temple
I have been told this
I believe it

On terminology

the clinical definition of gender dysphoria
is psychological distress
resulting from a difference between sex
assigned at birth
and gender identity

personally
I would say it results more
from the *assigning*
than the sex

I like my body
I like my slender wrists
my long fingers
the slight dip in of my waist
and the slight curve out of my stomach

and I don't mind
how those things result
from a set of hormones and chromosomes
under my skin
in my skin
my brain
inextricable from my self

what I don't like
is the word *breasts*

my chest
itself
is not the issue
it's the way you look at it
and draw a thousand little conclusions
that I can never really stamp out

I don't mind *tits*
less gendered
somehow
in its crude sexuality

maybe that's because blokes say tits
maybe that gives me
(bloke-adjacent)
some right to the word
maybe if I objectify myself sufficiently
I will go so far outside this assigned self
that you actually see me

hey man
look at me
self-contained gender binary
oppressing myself?
maybe!

hey boy
can I be your boyfriend
with the girlfriend implications?
if you wanna match me
I'll shout you the dress

don't suppose I could borrow it
once or twice?

play dress-up
strip my binder off like I'm stuffing a bra
for my own invisible drag show
make that assigned destiny
as shallow as pirates and mermaids
swipe it off with makeup wipes
when I'm done playing
strip back down to something un-assigned
un-performed
flesh and blood and shining eyes
and still get a kiss after?

could you call me pretty
like it's something that I shouldn't be
and mean it?

Good representation

I want to write you a poem
without it turning into a thesis
just one poem
just for you

I want to tell you I love you
without a campaign third-wheeling
without needing to defend it
without begging them to let me

I want to say *I love you*
without saying *despite it all*
without saying *whatever they think*
without saying *and I'm not ashamed of it*

I should not need to say these things
I should be able to say *I'll keep you safe*
and mean only *from monsters,*
from the dark

I should not have to wonder
if it's romantic
to know that I might die for this
and love you anyway

I want to scream it from the rooftops
and have it mean only itself
hold your hand in the street
and not think of the message we're sending

I want to talk about your eyes, your laugh,
pomegranate tea with too much honey,
all the things that don't win us sympathy-
I want this poem to be about you

I love you
I'm sorry I can't leave it at that

Nonpoem

poetic love is so often violence
love is war, is agony
love tears you apart and you die for it
and it's worth it
because it's love

maybe I don't want a poem
I would rather tea and biscuits
gentle words and late nights
I don't want it to hurt

there are enough poems
about the ways that this might end us
enough of regret, of misdirected hate
of our bodies ill-fitting and inescapable
enough of the stories where we succumb
in the end
to the picket fence dream
and the author claims a trophy

I like the one
where I have scars on my chest
when I tell you I love you
and you kiss me like nothing else but this
and we stay
just like that
for as long as we like
and there is no ending

Worship

there is nothing holy to me in suffering
self-inflicted pain
or righteous sacrifice

I make coffee
I read
I peel oranges
I watch the birds

worship is this

death will not redeem me
my best friend is laughing at something I said
because I didn't die yesterday

I reshape myself
I make my body fit me
I redecorate my room
I keep breathing

worship is this

humans can make angels of our better natures
our hopes
a bit of imagination

I eat
I dream
I love

I am alive

worship is this

Act IV

contains queerphobia, fear of hate crimes, internalised
ableism, and discussion of death

Sunset

when I was fifteen
I watched a sunset for the first time
and I cried

I know
fifteen is a little late for that
my mother did try
and so did I

when I was younger
I saw the sun set
and my brain buzzed impatience
as I nailed my feet to the ground
pinned my eyes open
and tried to find what the others were seeing

it still ended in tears
sometimes
frustrated burning at the corners of my eyes
nails biting into palms
> *focus, damnit*
> *you're missing it*
> *you're doing it wrong*
but a sunset never filled me up enough
to spill over

when I was fifteen
I had my earbuds in
humming smoke to the bees
and I didn't need pins
or nails

I sat on a beach
I watched a sunset
and I cried

Formacine

if there is something greater
it does not know me
could not
any more than I could know
the inner workings of a butterfly

imagine explaining marriage to an ant
when you love someone very much,
you say, *sometimes you promise them forever*
and the ant asks,
love?

still, here I am, incomprehensible
in my tiny fragile body
vibrating the air with laughter
brushing soft fingers over papercuts
and watching the stars

something out there plays with planets like marbles
swirls nebulas like paint in water
the ants fuss over cracks in tunnels
too small for my eyes to see

and all the while
I eat apples in a school library
and I think about eternity

Protostar

so it goes like this:
you're sixteen years old,
fresh out of quarantine
new school, new you,
new eyeshadow, new black nails

new bright-eyed kid
staring up at you
saying *hi! I, uh- I just-*
what are your pronouns?

and you're realising
you never once got to ask that question
before you knew your own answer

and you're saying
  he/hi-
  he/it
with a little injoke-building grin

and they're saying
  they/the-
  it/they
like this might just be the first time

so it goes like this:
you're sixteen years old
and you're witnessing the birth of a star
and you don't know what the hell to say to it
so you just grin a little wider
and let them in on your name

Risk Assessment

you ever hear a kid say
I don't care if they kill me?

let's play pretend for a moment
picture them
bright eyes, big hoodie
put the words in their mouth
let them say it with conviction

they mean it
you know
you meant it
it's funny with the right crowd –
dressed to get myself killed!

last week you bought your best friend makeup
and taught her how to wear it
took her out for the evening like a gentleman
and stuck to the crowded streets

when the boy in the car screamed at you
you gripped her hand tight to stop yours shaking
stuck your tongue out
and laughed until she joined in

there were pins on your backpack
that you turned it over to hide
alone on the train the next morning
dressed for the gender on the ticket

here's your secret —
you care if they kill you

the kid's thirteen

what do you say?

Countertops

I'm growing up
onward, along
stretched out like taffy
startled for a moment
to look down
and see the countertops
where my mother put the chocolate up
when I'd had too much

I learned from her how to stop myself
because she knew, then
how to take care of me
how to solve any trouble my little hands could reach

I can reach a lot further now
I know how to deal with chocolate
I don't know if she can teach me how to handle the universe
or put it safely on the top shelf

I don't know if she can teach me
how to teach myself
what's right
what's least-wrong
how to pick my battles
how to pick the *right* ones, and fight them right
how to understand that people can be so difficult
and complicated
and ignorant
and still be good

I don't know if she knows
I wish she did
so she could pick me up
and tell me to stop panicking
because all I have to do is be honest
and everything will sort itself out

people don't like honesty anymore
but my mother never taught me how to lie
and the deep end of the pool has never been as kind a teacher
even when you jump in yourself

a lovely thing about my mother –
even when she did
she doesn't *say* 'I told you so'

maybe we'll work the next one out together

6,662 days in

I don't think there is a heaven
I wish I did
there are people I love who never knew my name
and I would like to tell them

I don't think we were designed to be alive
or to know it will end
to see ourselves as electrical impulses
forming a pattern by chance for an instant

at most moments in time
I do not exist to think about it
most things happen without me
I am lucky to get this long

I would say
any less would be unbearable
but if I had any longer
I would say the same

this little is not bearable
but if I do not bear it
I will waste it
and that is far worse

so I will bear it
I will watch the sun set
and allow myself to be distracted
by the spiders in the grass

and until there isn't, I will trust
that there will be another sunset
another sunrise
another spider

I will trust that I can spare the time
because if I do not spare it
I will waste it
and that is far worse

there is nothing after this
so this will have to be enough
we can make it enough
we have the time

there is time for tea
and books
and aimless kisses

there is time for spiders
and sunsets
and poems about them

I am an accident
and within a century
I will be nothing at all

what reason more do I need?

Coda

...and he never quite stops wondering
but it's *to be*

About the author

Born to folk musicians, Oliver Roweth (he/it) grew up in a small town on Wiradjuri land and at a variety of folk festivals all over NSW. Between storytelling, music, poetry, and many, many trips to the library, language has always been the lens through which he views the world.

Performing bush poetry on festival stages from the age of six, Oliver began to write its own freeverse poems in early highschool. Throughout its teenage years, writing has been a way to both process its experiences and share the parts of them that can feel almost impossible to explain.

Oliver is currently studying English Literature and Sociology at the University of Wollongong. He has come to realise that the long and messy process of growing up never really ends, and fully expects to continue writing diary entries with line breaks until the day he dies.